MOUNTAIN *to* VALLEY

Mountain to Valley

Poems for your Path

Mark Miles

Xulon Press

Xulon Press Elite
2301 Lucien Way #415
Maitland, FL 32751
407.339.4217
www.xulonpress.com

© 2023 by Mark Miles

All rights reserved solely by the author. The author guarantees all contents are original and do not infringe upon the legal rights of any other person or work. No part of this book may be reproduced in any form without the permission of the author.

Due to the changing nature of the Internet, if there are any web addresses, links, or URLs included in this manuscript, these may have been altered and may no longer be accessible. The views and opinions shared in this book belong solely to the author and do not necessarily reflect those of the publisher. The publisher therefore disclaims responsibility for the views or opinions expressed within the work.

Paperback ISBN-13: 9781662871771
Ebook ISBN-13: 9781662871788

Dedication:

There are so many whom I need to thank for their love and support in the writing of this book. First and foremost is my Lord and Savior, Jesus Christ, who gave the words and thoughts for these poems. He alone deserves all the glory for all whose lives will be changed from this collection.

The second is my wife, Cheryl, whose love and support gave me the strength and belief to complete this project. In my life, I am truly blessed from the power and love of both!

To my family and friends who have shared their thoughts and prayers about this book, you are an inspiration, and my prayer is that you are blessed as much by this book as I am by your friendship. Thank you all!

Preface:

In this world, there are many paths we can take to get to our destination. Some will allow us to walk without tough decisions or delays. Yet sometimes, God allows a different path to show us something that we need to experience. Our walk on these paths lead to mountain experiences, where the climb is difficult but the reward, when complete, is worth the effort. Sometimes we are to walk a valley path that can be dark and dry with no idea of its direction. But God uses both to show a glimpse of where He wants us to go.

This book was written for all pilgrims who are walking on their path to eternity. God has given each of us the opportunity to seek Him in the chaos of this world. My hope is for you to find comfort and His peace in these poems. They were placed on my heart to share with you to help you on your path.

Mark

Table of Contents

Dedication v
Preface vii
The Rewards 1
Family Night 2
Year's Dawning 3
Time Passage 4
Moriah's Test 6
God's Choice 8
Son's Call 9
Faithful Heart 10
Morning Call 12
Faith Storms 14
Written Choices 15
Storm Watch 16
True Wealth 17
Jerusalem Communion 18
Gethsemane Choices 20
Heaven's Host 21
Hope Begins 23
The Victory 24
Our Plan 26
Morning Walk 28
Pilgrim's Race 29
Spirit Wind 30
Aged Armor 31
Believer's Path 32
Conflict Strong 33
Daylight's Visit 34
Emmanuel Chosen 35
Faith's Victory 36

God's Harbor	37
Heaven Sounds	38
Knowing God	39
Life's Tapestry	41
Mountain Mist	42
New Walk	43
Prayerful Meeting	44
Strength Unfolded	45
Quiet Time	46
Visions Past	47
Welcome Host	48
Morning Voice	49
New Chance	50
Friends Gathered	51
Angel Watch	52
Crossroad Choices	53
Night Fights	54
Heaven's Gain	55
Daily Challenge	56
Portrait Drawn	57
Memories Visions	58
Love's Legacy	59
Nights Together	60
God Revealed	61
Chosen Hearts	62
Hilltop Renewal	63
Timeless Shield	64
Heaven's Hope	66
Morning Test	67
Love's Fight	68
Night Light	69
First Day	70
God's Freedom	71
Homecoming Rest	72
Choose Joy	73
Heaven's Home	74

Morning Visit	75
New Home	76
Finished Work	77
Gifts Given	78
Heart Unfolded	79
Daily Fight	81
Houses of Light	82
New Song	83
Heaven's Race	84
Choosing Thanks	85
Grandpa's Treasure	86
Majestic Walk	88
Reality's Dream	89
Paused Power	90
Eternal Choice	91
Nature Walk	92
Morning to Evening	93
Wilderness Walked	94
Heaven's Gate	95
New Voice	96
Published Works	97
Heart Songs	99
Morning Peace	101
Heart Talks	102
Waves of Grace	103
God's Gift	104
Mother's Love	105
Mary's Hope	106
Heaven's Gift	107
Christmas Shadow	108
Heavenly Journey	110
Emmanuel's Gift	111
Stable Rest	112
Beautiful Choice	113
Seasons Together	115

The Rewards

Lord, what is this gift
You have given to me,
The wonder of words
Painting pictures to see?

The things of my heart
That I dare not say,
You have allowed me to write
As a verse through the day.

I do not know the reason
You gave me this gift.
But Lord, help those souls,
Of the needy, to lift.

And Lord, may I pray
As I write the words down,
That lost souls are saved
And from You receive crowns.

Family Night

The windowpanes are an artist's dream
With murals painted white.
We sit while the fireplace warms the room
This cold and wintry night.

Our family joins in simple fun;
We play and reminisce old times.
It seems so hard to stop and rest
Our hurried pace in life.

To see our daughter laugh with glee
At old pictures once more seen.
We've changed the pace from slow to fast,
The past life just a dream.

Now sitting here, we stop to talk
And share our thoughts and fears.
With wintry storms painting landscapes white,
We embrace with mingling tears.

So now this cold and blustery night,
Our home's been touched anew.
We'll slow our pace and enjoy the walk
Since we have but one time through.

Year's Dawning

The dawn broke clear on this frosty morn
As its rays chased the night away.
I stirred as the light entered the room,
Such a beautiful start to my day.

It is the birth of a new year for pilgrims
As we seek out the way for our lives.
What changes will come from the Master
To bring joy or maybe some strife.

In our world, we can see only heartache
As the focus of man seems so dark.
Our lives tend to sway like those lost ones.
Can we listen to what's in our heart?

When we gave up life's sin that enslaved us
To get victory sure through the blood,
Why do we keep lives so entangled
With the world we once so loved?

This pilgrim once struggled with life there
Till he found out the way for those here.
For the saved, there is no path here worthy.
Only His way can ring in the year!

Time Passage

The morning mist hung all around,
Giving shadowy places life.
When, from the distance, familiar sounds
Of his Maker's steady strides.

In a moment's time, he turned to see
This one so pure and bright.
Through the rustling grass, Adam saw
His God, such a wondrous sight.

Still farther down the path in time,
Another waited for Him.
A small lad tended sheep and goats
On a hill outside Bethlehem.

One night he awoke to glorious sounds
From overhead as the anthems rang.
The songs so beautiful, telling all
Of the Savior's birth, they sang.

Yet even farther down that path,
We arrive at our present day
And wake to strive with all around,
Not listening for what the Lord might say.

You see, my friend, I think it's time
To rest in a shady place
With expectant hearts so tuned to Him
That we know when we see His face.

It may not be on a misty morn
Or a hill where angels sing.
But friend, you will know if you invite Him in,
For your life will never be the same!

Moriah's Test

The night air was crisp as they loaded, then left
To seek out the place for the test.
Each pack mule and camel bore the pieces he'd use,
For the sacrifice must be the best.

In the light of dawn, Abraham led all those there
Toward a place not yet known, far ahead.
Each day brought them closer to the path two would walk
Up a mount to the altar, then death.

He stopped at the foot and left all others there;
Just he and young Isaac would go on.
They gathered the wood and the tools they would use.
Abraham loaded the wood on his son.

As they climbed, Abraham wondered of promises made,
How his seed would be as grains of sand.
Their steps labored up to find there the place,
An altar and sacrifice from his hands.

Stores gathered, wood piled, and his son bound, then laid
As a lamb to be slain for his Lord.
The knife was raised high to slay the boy there.
In that moment, Abraham heard the Angel's words.

"Touch not the boy, for your test pleases me.
In this way, your love's proved for all time.
Look away from the altar to that bush by the rock;
I have given you the sacrificial lamb."

The story we know, and its promises are true
But I wonder what each said when it was done.
Did Isaac grow angry, was Abraham sad? I think not,
For the play they'd lived out was like God's Son!

So there on Moriah, God gave us a view,
What His Son would bear for the world.
Wood carried, hill climbed, and blood spilled on the ground;
Perfect sacrifice, sin's debt paid, greatest story told!

God's Choice

The sun beat down on the young man's face
  As the voice of God came near.
  "Joshua, rise and take the lead.
  Moses is now with me, do not fear."

  Standing now, he took his place
To lead God's people to their new home.
  How could it be that he was the one?
Yet in God's power, he would not be alone.

Have you stood and looked at a wilderness
  That seems much too hard to go through?
  With little strength and hope to match,
    What will you choose to do?

When we stand before a wall that is strong,
But God says, "Walk on and just trust me."
  I choose to trust and follow on a path,
  Knowing God will be there to lead.

It is seldom here that our path is smooth
  As Satan tries to inflict all those here.
  Still the power of God, our living hope,
  Brings us through in His power so dear.

Son's Call

The young boy played as his father worked
With sawdust and chips all around.
His smile beamed as his father looked down
To the son, now content, with wood found.

In time, the father trained his son,
For he would also work with the wood.
So great was his love for his father
That he learned and performed the best he could.

The time soon came that the Son felt His call.
From the Father, He had left for this time.
Jesus left His home to follow the path
That His Father had given Him to climb.

In those years, Jesus worked to bring to us
A picture of Emmanuel and His love.
People saw in the man a portrait of God
Who had been sent from heaven above.

Seeing Jesus work with the people
In their lives, He instilled peace and joy.
Fulfilling His calling in His death on the cross,
Our hope was delivered from that boy!

Faithful Heart

The sun bore down through cloudless skies
    As the young lad slowed his pace.
His sweating brow was streaked with dust
    When he wiped his heated face.

With food and clothes, his father gave,
    David's journey was almost done.
Just one more hill to climb atop
    To bring the supplies to Jesse's sons.

Then startled suddenly by a shout
    From the other valley near,
The young boy ran to see the event
    And the reason for this cheer.

He gasped as he saw a man so huge
    That he seemed just like a tree.
Yet looking past this crazy sight
    Were the armies of Saul the king.

With hurried steps, David went around,
    Making his way into the camp.
His face showed pain and breathing hard;
    He asked where his brothers would stand.

The shouts and cheers were turned to darts
As they hurled them all at Saul.
"Why don't we fight?" young David asked
Still, none would heed his call.

Yet when Goliath cursed the God
Of Israel and these men,
The youngest lad in all the camp
Gave the Lord the chance to win.

You see, the lad didn't see the man
As an overwhelming foe
But just a way for Jehovah's name
And true power to be shown.

So, in that valley, hot and dry,
A lad who was put to the test
Proved to all the strength of faith
And that His Lord was truly best.

Morning Call

The night was long as they worked the nets,
Trying hard for a catch so in need.
With payments due and family near,
Only work through the night, they'd agreed.

Stars above shown on water still
Kept them working through the night.
Yet dawn's embrace left saddened face,
For the men in the boats were in sight.

Ashore they came with their nets to clean,
Then go home with nothing for those there.
Each worked in silence to just get done,
Wanting to rest with no story to share.

Jesus stood and turned to see them near,
And He approached just to borrow their boat.
His people could hear so much better from there.
Peter stood, looked at Jesus, then said:

"We have little time now, teacher; take them away,
For our work through the night gave no gain."
Jesus drew Peter in, then said once again,
"In your effort and plan, you've only pain."

Peter's shoulders shrugged hard as he pushed out the boat
To a sea that held from them last night.
"Cast your net once again; just try it," and then
Loads of fish and Messiah were in sight.

Faith Storms

The boat was tossed by the wind that night,
And those men were struck with such fear.
In the storm, they could see the end of their life.
Widened eyes could have held desperate tears.

Then they turned back to see Him there fast asleep
With a face that did not see the storm.
He awoke as they screamed of the death they now faced.
"Why the doubt, this can bring you no harm."

Every day we face battles that rage ever near,
Where we choose fear or faith in the fight.
Just as the disciples in the boat with the storm,
Still the Master's power was shown there that night.

What you face daily, only look to the one
Whose words stilled the fear in their hearts.
He ordered the wind and the waves to obey.
"Peace, be still" caused the storm to depart.

I have struggled like you with storms in the night
So dark that no light could be seen.
Only Jesus can calm and bring peace in your storm,
A gift to be given by Him!

Written Choices

The woman knelt as the crowd drew near
With anger hot and stones in hands.
She was guilty with no doubt left to speak.
Her life would soon end from these men.

It was at that moment God came near,
Not in thunder or a lightning bolt,
But in a simple teacher who knelt to write.
The crowd, incensed, began to shout.

Jesus paused and stooped to write in the dust,
Which began to melt the enraged crowd's heart.
Not knowing what he wrote, they stood;
Each one played an important part.

The crowd was hushed as Jesus spoke,
Never looking at any man there.
"Let him without sin cast the first stone."
The crowd dropped the stones in despair.

"Where are your accusers?" Jesus asked the girl,
For the men had dropped the stones, then left.
The woman was given a new start that day
To live out her life in His gift.

So many years have passed since that day,
Yet the story and promise are true.
If we will just open the door to our heart,
Jesus comes in and makes our life new!

Storm Watch

The waves lapped gently against the boat
As the disciples loaded their gear.
With seasoned men, they pushed out at last,
Going to the other side and waiting for Him there.

Jesus went to the mountain to talk to His Father
When a storm so intense engulfed all of them.
So great was the wind that they could not sail
As the waves washed over the men.

The Master saw the danger and walked to the sea,
Yet the waves had no effect on the Lord.
He walked without fear, for the storm could not harm,
But He saw in their faces greater storms.

It was then that they saw a strange form coming close.
Peter called out to see what it could be.
The Master spoke boldly to comfort them,
For they knew He could calm angry seas.

Have you been in a storm where your heart feared?
It is not for the weak to embrace.
But the redeemed know the storm poses no harm
Since, in its fury, I see only His face.

True Wealth

The morning sun was warming them
When a young man came to talk.
His heart was strong with a life to match.
He was known by the Master for his walk.

With riches gained and a life lived well,
For he followed the Scriptures each day,
He leaned in close as Jesus drew near,
Yet he could not have dreamed what He'd say.

"If you want to be free and be in heaven with me,
Go and give all your riches away."
Then the young man stopped, his head bowed low.
In that moment, he knew he couldn't stay.

My friend, do the things that you have earned in life
Bring you a sense of security and ease?
It was for that young man who left Jesus that day.
So, look again at how deeply they please.

Our Father looks down as we live our lives,
And He sees where our treasure lies.
True riches rest now where we will be blessed
When we reach heaven's home at His side.

Jerusalem Communion

The day had been long and tiresome
As they walked Jerusalem's streets;
So many people pressing near
This Jesus just to meet.

He stood amidst the growing throng
With all He loved so dear.
His entry to the precious place
To His disciples seemed so clear.

They knew that soon He would proclaim to all
The place where He would stand.
Yet when they asked when was the time,
Jesus raised a gentle hand.

"It is not time to speak of this,"
He said as He stood upright.
Then moving slowly to a bowl,
He wrapped a towel around tight.

He knelt before those in the room
And washed their feet so slow.
With words they could not understand,
Jesus said He soon must go.

The puzzled looks on each man's face
Gave their Master more to say.
With cautious words, He spoke of pain
and the price He would have to pay.

Then with a cup, the Master spoke
Of blood spilled for the cost.
The bread He broke was of His body dear
To pay sin's price for the lost.

With their time now drawing to a close,
They rose to go and pray.
Yet now we know the price Christ paid
And have freedom though our day.

You see, with the cup and bread, He showed
That His life would soon be spent.
But when His grave was opened up,
He gave us the way to repent!

Gethsemane Choices

The hills and paths were growing dark
As they made their way that night.
Up to the mountain, they quietly walked,
For Gethsemane was not yet in sight.

Finally reaching the garden, they entered.
Jesus told the men to just wait.
Then looking back, He chose three men
To go with Him as the hour grew late.

In time they stopped; Jesus looked around
To a night so cold and dark.
He asked them to pray, then went on alone
Just for a time with His Father to talk.

Reaching a place where He could pray,
Jesus poured out His heart there alone.
With drops, as blood, coming down His face,
His petitions were sent to God's throne.

Yet even in silence, Jesus's Father spoke,
For His Son must go through with their plan.
The pain and death would now soon begin;
This was why He was sent to save man!

Heaven's Host

The host of heaven all held their breath
As the Son was beaten, then bound.
His life had been pure and given to those
Who watched yet uttered no sound.

The man in the robe gave a choice for those there
To free just one man on that day.
Then a sense of confusion crept into the host,
And they all had nothing to say.

When the crowd gave its choice, Pilate stood yet again.
In hushed tone, he levied his words.
Release now Barabbas; take the teacher once more
To scourge Him and crown Him with thorns.

Over rough streets, He carried the cross for a time,
Then collapsed at the weight that bore down.
On His face was the pain He had suffered alone
With the blood from His beatings and crown.

He looked up to see the way of the cross.
Its streets filled with shouts and with tears.
Our Savior continued to Golgotha's hill
With a purpose that never showed fear.

Then the silence in heaven gave way to a gasp
As the Son was lifted on high.
His body now stretched and nailed to the cross
Left there just to suffer and die.

"It is finished," He said, and the host stood again,
For they could not have known of God's plan.
Jesus died for the price that we couldn't pay.
Through His blood, now there's hope for all men.

Hope Begins

The dawn broke through as night gave way
To a morning You had known would come.
Were there birds on high in the sky's bright hues
When Your beatings and trial were done?

How steep were the steps on Your way that day
As the Lamb made His way to the tree?
Your cross bore down and pushed that crown
Where Your blood flowed down in the street.

What did You see as they raised Your cross?
Could You see all Your accusers there?
In Your pain, were there thoughts of finishing now?
For Your purpose would complete without fear.

When Your Father turned away and our sin laid on You,
Did You struggle with its weight that bore down?
Still, You reached out to Him, only finding the sin.
It was for this that You laid down Your crown.

Then with victory sure from the battle that raged,
You held the keys that kept us bound.
In Your triumph, You began the true hope for all men.
The tomb opened, and man's hope now was found.

The Victory

I wonder how bad
You felt on that day
When all your disciples
Had run far away.

Your heart must have been
Too heavy to bear.
The burden of sin
For mankind, You would wear.

The trial and the mocking,
I am sure, brought such grief.
Just the thought of the end
Should have given relief.

But the feelings You had
Were of soon-coming pain,
For the death of Messiah
Would be for man's gain.

From that cross on Golgotha,
You started the plan.
That Your shed blood would cover
The sins of all men.

Then soon came the morning
When they went to the grave.
They found the tomb empty.
Now from death, we are saved.

Our Plan

The people were gathered
In the courtyard that day.
Awaiting the decision
Of what Pilate would say.

He found the man blameless,
Yet still gave the choice
For this man to go free.
We screamed, "No!" with one voice.

So, he gave the man over
To be beaten and bound.
They hurt Him so badly,
Yet He uttered no sound.

Then with thorns cutting deep
From the crown soldiers gave,
He carried His cross
To Golgotha that day.

We watched as they drove
Those cold spikes in His hands.
Then raised up His cross
Was the end of our plan.

I watched Him grow weak
From His torment and pain.
Yet I had a strange feeling
That this all was in vain.

Then I watched Him and heard
As He breathed His last breath.
"It is finished," He said.
And with that, He was dead.

We should have been joyful
That this man was now gone.
But at death, the ground shook
And clouds darkened the sun.

For three days, we feared
That His words had been true.
Then we found His grave empty,
And too late, then we knew.

That our plan was accomplished,
Not for our gain, we see.
He was fulfilling God's promise
With Christ's blood on the tree.

Morning Walk

The demons gathered 'round and gave raspy sounds
 As the body was placed in the tomb.
Your battle began as You gave Your life's blood for man.
Then the stone rolled, and Your sentence was done.

When men walked away, all Your loved ones stayed
 In Your death, they could find no hope.
Still, the real battle began as You fought for all men,
 So the prize of the keys could be won.

The days in the tomb were for hope now to come,
 For in Your victory, all men have a choice.
With sin and death done, You woke as His Son
In that tomb, where their shouts became a stilled voice.

A new day was born as You walked out that morn.
Was Your stride as it was when You were king?
Where the prisons of sin destroyed for all time?
 How beautiful was the Son-rise that day?

In Your battle, You won as God's only Son,
 And Your victory gave Your Father sweet peace.
Restored now on high, and for man's sin, You died.
 All nature rested in the hope now released.

Pilgrim's Race

I read today about the life of Paul.
His words brought sweet joy to my heart.
In that cell so dark and cold, he lived,
Waiting for his heavenly journey to start.

He wrote to us of the race he was in
And how he longed to finish it strong.
With a life lived out in the power of Christ
In a world where he did not belong.

That race he ran is still with us today.
Each must compete in the power of Him.
It is not in our strength that the race is run,
For in Jesus, the victory, we will win!

So run now, dear friend, and fight for the prize,
From the one whose race was won.
He will guide you today and give you His strength
Till that moment when to heaven you have come.

Your trials and victories now complete;
Rest in the victory you have won.
When there, we will all be given our crown
That we will lay at the feet of the Son!

Spirit Wind

The upper room was strangely quiet
As they opened hearts to pray.
It had been some time since Jesus left.
Still, they knew what He had said.

A comforter strong and sure would come
Yet they could not know just when.
So, in that room so quiet and still,
Heartfelt prayers were offered to Him.

In that moment, a sound came drawing near.
It came in power as a rushing wind,
Enveloping all that gathered there
And settling on those within.

In all years passing from that upper room,
The Spirit still works His power,
Giving each believer His special strength
To sustain us in our darkest hour.

So, rest now, friend, your need is seen
By the one who watches overall.
His love and strength will guide us on
And will keep us even when we fall.

Aged Armor

The day dawned clear for the aged man.
In his pain, he opened his eyes.
Once again, he stretched to begin his day
With the fight close, he had to try.

His armor lay around him there.
Its look was diminished by time.
So many scars on the armor now;
He had fought and held the line.

He stood again and began to dress
For the battle stood at the door.
Without the strength that the armor gave,
No fight could be fought anymore.

In his suit, he stood and glanced again
At the sight of a warrior grown old.
A mind still sharp and softened heart
Held his story that he knew should be told.

Today he will face a fight so strong
That no one could withstand on their own.
But with armor on and shield held high,
In God's strength, the victory will be won.

We all have a story that must be shared
To generations that need to hear.
Put your armor on and win the fight,
Then tell the story to all you hold dear.

Believer's Path

You talked today of paths you've walked
In your "old man's shoes," you trod.
Then hearing words, your heart was changed
As if by the hand of God.

With each new day, your spirit grew
In the knowledge of Christ, the Son.
The old ways waned as your path then changed,
Many victories having been won.

Yet now your path seems hard to walk.
The joy has left your life.
You plod along each long hard day
With overwhelming strife.

My friend, our prayer is for your time
To be spent resting in Him,
Who changed your path that day long past
And saved you from your sin.

He'll lift you high to soar again
As you rest in Him above.
His glory to hold and carry you on
When you trust and rest in His love.

Conflict Strong

The day was hot and dry
As we walked along that day
Among the many tombstones,
Giving homage to the brave.

We followed down the paths
Where the bravest of the brave
Gave all they had to offer
Just to end up in a grave.

Yet while I walked those fields,
Your Spirit spoke to me.
Of the war that we fight daily
With a foe we cannot see.

Even now the foe advances
To take us unaware.
His way of fighting battles
Is anything but fair.

But with all our trouble fighting,
We know the victory is sure,
For our weakness is perfected.
With Your power, we're secure.

So, the foe retreats, now beaten
By our overpowering Lord!
With Satan gone forever,
Slain by Jesus's holy sword.

Daylight's Visit

The dawn broke cold, crisp, and clear
With the first light of the beautiful day.
My aging frame fought the early pain
As I looked for what the Lord had to say.

In those first few minutes, with my mind so quiet
And my heart peaceful and still,
His Word bore witness of power and grace.
In my spirit, His presence I could feel.

Why is it, friend, that the peace Jesus gives
Seems to wane with the pace of our life?
It's in Him we find joy and comfort sublime,
In His strength, a shield from all strife.

Yet each day here brings new hardships to bear.
In their grasp, we fight to get free.
For all in that moment must ponder, then pause
Just looking for the escape to be seen.

Our Jesus is stronger than the hardships we face.
His Word brings us power and love.
We must only be still and search deeply His Word
There to find His strength from above.

Emmanuel Chosen

In the morning light, I thought of you
And the choice you chose to make,
To leave your home so rich and sweet
For the world that You had made.

A path not easy for You to trod,
For to start, You must give up Your place.
In the choice You made, your course was set,
Where the world could see God's face.

It wasn't a palace so grand to see
Where You made Your entrance here.
But a stable small and dimly lit,
You were born with Mary's tears.

So now we sit in rooms each day,
Brightly lit with the lights on trees.
And in that light, if we stop and look,
We'll see a hill called Calvary.

Your decision was made without any fear,
So our lives could be given a choice.
With softened lights and hearts to match,
If we choose, we can hear God's voice.

Faith's Victory

The sands of time are moving
To a sound that no man can hear.
Each move of their grains is chosen
by the Lord, His ways to make clear.

Our world is ablaze with a warfare
That impacts all our lives in its fire.
What chance do we have to reach safety
From these armies, never seeming to tire?

So, stop, friend, and rest in His promise
Given there on a dark starry night.
The battle that rages around us
Is not one we're intended to fight.

A plan was delivered in a stable
To a young girl to bring forth a Son.
His name would be Jesus, the Savior,
And the war for our world was now won.

The answer now given was simple.
Just believe and accept what was done.
Emmanuel, God with us, empowered;
Our world would be won by the Son!

God's Harbor

As the waves come crashing over the walls,
What holds you in your place?
When storms rage on, around your life,
Is there a frown upon your face?

While strong seas here engulf all those
Who you call your loved ones dear,
Do you fight to help them stay afloat
Until they are safely clear?

My friend, when storms around us rage,
With waves and seas so high,
The only harbor safe to rest
Is the one where God is nigh.

Our Father holds us safely in
His harbor sheltered safe.
Though seas are rough around us there,
Only calm seas fill this place.

So, when your boat is tossed and blown
By life's storms rough and long.
Sail to the harbor, where God dwells.
His power will calm the storm.

Heaven Sounds

The hallowed halls of time speak loudly
Of the times when Jesus came near.
His works and words have stood time's test
Just to make our way more clear.

Within that barn, the first sound came
From the beautiful newborn babe.
In His early years, he proved to all
That the manger was where Emmanuel laid.

Once more, a sound comes 'round us now
Of the Master's work in Cana.
Again, time's halls picked up the sound
In the tears and cheers for Messiah.

Again, the sounds come sweeping through
It is the sound of hammer and nails.
A cross raised high, then left to die;
Hammers rings, the story tells.

Yet now we know the gift He brings
Is a story that all must know.
From humble birth to loving feasts
To a cross, then tomb He chose.

Knowing God

Throughout all time, a debate has raged
Of just how a man sees God.
In all this battle's fiercest fight,
No winner has been found.

Some men see God as a provider still,
Handing out some service here.
Till through some circumstance all is gone,
They're left kneeling in their tears.

Others see God as heartless and cruel;
Their sin burden weighs heavily down.
They can't see God as any good,
Much less to see His crown.

Still others see Him as a means
To gain all that they can.
When riches fade, they have no choice;
Their faith has been in man.

Yet when I walk a meandering stream
And feel its rushing power
Or gaze upon a mountain range,
Watching eagles as they soar.

It is clear to see how real God is
When you know who holds in place
Each tiny part that plays its role
On our planet hung in space.

You see, my friend, our world goes on;
Each day given over by Him,
Who loved us all so clearly
That His Son's blood paid for our sin.

No man can tell me God's not real,
For I know what all can find.
To see our God for what He is,
Look to your heart, friend, not your mind.

Life's Tapestry

It came so softly to my heart
With a touch so soft and pure.
I wasn't looking for this thing,
Yet its purpose here was sure.

Within the time it takes to blink,
My Father placed His Word.
There wasn't any symbol crash
Or a sound that could be heard.

He spoke of a beautiful tapestry
That we all have helped to make.
Each daily task is woven there
As our picture soon takes shape.

Those tasks you do throughout your day
Have spun a daily scene.
Your deeds done well or poorly worked
Lend a purpose to be seen.

So, friend, I pray you will take some time
To see what part you will play.
That all those lost who see your work
Will see Christ's love through the day.

Mountain Mist

The mist now seen begins to move
In the shadows of my life.
It bears within the past I have built
With its joy and some with strife.

I follow Him as He guides me true
On a path never seen before.
His gentle ways I understand
As I search for what is in store.

In view, I see a mountain tall,
The path too steep to climb.
Yet in His hands, I begin my trek
To its peak for so short a time.

With views to see where few have stood,
the beauty takes my breath away.
Still in that moment, His gentle nudge,
But I stand, just wanting to stay.

His arms now hold as we look below
To a valley so dark and long.
We begin our descent in the growing mist
In His grip that has been proven strong.

New Walk

Throughout my life, I have looked behind
At my rags of sin tossed away.
Their stench was strong and filled with tears
That I had shed most every day.

Yet in my sin, I knew there was more
To bring joy and peace to my life.
Then I met the one who had come for me.
In His sacrifice, He paid the price.

For on that cross, as He hung so high,
Neither heaven nor earth could hold.
His righteous life and sinless death
Gave a story that must be told.

So, friend, your choice is just as mine
To accept or reject His plan.
Its perfect price was paid for all
When His blood spilled out for man.

Each day I stop and look once more
At my path behind through time.
Now within each mile, only beauty is seen.
All those sins, I cannot find.

Prayerful Meeting

Where do you go when the world crashes down?
It is part of our journey not knowing just when.
For when the world calls you, how do you answer,
With a frown etched deep or a wink and grin?

You see, friend, I have learned over the years
That this world holds our path for a time.
The walk can be steep and dark on some days,
But we can endure in its grasp on the climb.

While valleys are dark and shrouded from view,
In our steps, we can trust the one who gives grace.
His power will hold and keep you safe
As we walk in His peace as He leads.

Your heart will be challenged in the steps here today,
But its challenge cannot do any harm.
With trials now surrounding, your heart yearns again
To run to the Lord's welcoming arms.

I rest often now at the foot of the cross,
For this world holds no place for me here.
At the cross, I meet the Lord daily in prayer,
Where my heart beats free from all earthly cares.

Strength Unfolded

In your times of darkest trial,
What speaks loudest to your heart?
It is in those words your course is set
To succeed or fail from the start.

Our life is fragile and must be held
With hands that show power and love.
To hold onto tight only imprisons our soul.
Open hands give us strength from above.

I have felt those cold fingers of gathering doom,
for in life, it is always waiting near.
We walk in this world amidst evil and good;
It is no wonder it easily brings tears.

But even when tossed by a trial in your soul,
You can see what the Lord wants to show.
His power and love will always be there,
Even when the purpose we won't know.

Rest now, child, and for the Son to come again
To all who need comfort and care.
Those powerful arms will enfold you, and yet,
He will restore you and help your load to bear.

Quiet Time

I sit alone most every day
Just to spend some time with You.
Our times are sweet, where hearts draw near.
Mine is touched, and, I hope, yours too.

Your love is deep, and I know it's true,
For I feel it throughout my day.
Once more, our time brings songs and tears
In that love, where I choose to stay.

Within my life, there were times of trial,
Where I fought for that deeper love.
Those times were fierce as fires raged within
To gain a peace that comes from God.

This world is at war within itself.
The greed and violence grows.
Yet in my heart, a peace is felt,
For the love from my King freely flows.

So, choose today to take time alone
And meet with the one who brings peace.
His love will fill your heart, and then
Your trials and pain you'll release.

Visions Past

My mind was spent when I thought of You
That, from eternity past, You had known;
The time and date of my life's events,
Where, from birth, You watched me grow.

Those times I tried but failed life's tests,
Yet You kept me in Your arms of grace.
To rise again when those tests returned;
In triumph, a smile came to my face.

What did You see in eternity past
That would cause this love in my heart?
How could it be that the image You saw
Would be grown in me from the start?

I know in that time, I felt Your call
To a heart that was darkened by sin.
Your Spirit was calling to a boy so lost.
Opened heart's door; brought a Savior within.

For most of my life, I have followed You here,
And my life has been blessed greater still.
It was in that image, You knew I would come
To give all my heart, strength, and will.

Welcome Host

Now in these walls, I rest assured
From the peace that I find within.
Still, others fight a continuous fight,
never knowing just how it will end.

What makes the two so different here
As the world engulfs them both?
It seems so small, but changes all,
For in your home, who is the host?

My heart was given so long ago
To the God who set me free.
In all my years, His presence is near,
Causing the world and its problems to flee.

You see, my friend, the home's not mine.
From His grace and blessings, He gave.
To believe it is mine would open doors
I know He closed to keep me safe.

So, friend, now rest if you are redeemed.
There is no home for you here, only heaven.
You can walk this world and enjoy its paths,
But your heart won't be free till you're there!

Morning Voice

Once more, I awoke to that still, small voice
Just to meet in our favorite place.
It is in the dark and quiet time
That it is easy to see Your face.

These days are filled with tumult strong.
Each fight takes our strength away.
When we look around at battles lost,
We find it hard to hear what You say.

This walk of faith has been one so long
With its valleys and mountains high.
In joy and pain, I move ever near
To Your side, where my spirit flies.

This world is failing at a faster pace
Than we have seen throughout our life.
Our leaders never meet the needs of all,
Giving no hope, only bringing strife.

So now in our time, my heart's weighed down,
For it is not in men we will find peace.
Your still, small voice brings that and more.
It is in Jesus that I have been set free!

New Chance

In my study time daily,
The Lord draws me near.
His words, though not spoken,
Are so easy to hear.

Your life, you live daily
In your thoughts, words, and deeds.
What purpose is served
For your love or your need.

If in your day you could stop
Just to see those around,
Their lives seem such a mess,
For their sin keeps them bound.

With lives held in shackles
From the weight of their sin,
Will you share your love freely
For their chance to find Him?

The words will flow clearly,
For the Spirit gives power.
A new chance is offered
To find Jesus that hour!

Friends Gathered

I feel the presence daily
Of my friend who is now passed.
The long and loving friendship
We shared until the last.

My mind brings pictures daily
Of his thoughtful ways for all.
He saw each person's purpose
And helped them when they'd fall.

I found myself in wonder
Of what he's doing now.
What sights he sees so lovely,
With no worry on his brow.

For you see my friends in heaven,
And I know I'll find him there.
At a supper prepared for believers,
Where their future is secure.

We'll all gather at the tables
To eat and worship with Him,
Who has saved us for eternity.
Through His blood, we're saved from sin!

Angel Watch

I walk each day in wars that rage,
For our world is ablaze in hate.
Each faction here stands ready to fight
When the enemy comes to the gate.

The servant of Elisha woke to this,
Then he went to his master in despair.
Encamped all around were armies of men.
Still, Elisha showed no fear with them there.

His prayer to the Lord opened the servant's eyes
To see not the armies of men.
But the hills and the valleys with chariots of fire,
Sent by God to watch over them.

Do you think, in our day, we are covered
By a host that were charged to protect?
Seeing those angels that stood on that hillside
Would give us a reason to never forget.

One day my eyes will be opened
To the ways that God used to guide.
His protection was sent down from heaven
Just to watch till we reach Jesus's side.

Crossroad Choices

I have often thought of the choices made
In that moment, where dreams are seen.
With uncertainty there, I made my way
To a road where I had never been.

On those paths that were chosen, I made my way,
Led secure in the Father's hands.
Some paths have been easy with beauty seen;
Yet on others, left alone there to stand.

My choices were made with a heart of prayer
And His strength to carry me through.
Yet some choices made were only my own
There to see failure that was all mine too.

You see, friend, in life, many crossroads are found
Just to build faith in the Father above.
From seeking His wisdom and finding His Word
To enrich all our life with His love.

So, rest now and look at the pathway you chose
And fulfill what our Lord has in store.
The strength of the Father will carry you through
Till you finally reach heaven's shore.

Night Fights

How long has it been since we held them close
And wiped all their tears away?
Much too fast they grew, then suddenly left,
Listening to what others might say.

It was in our faith that we prayed and led
Our children to prepare for their life.
With some, it grew with roots down deep,
Yet in others, disbelief brought much strife.

I know all too well the prayers lifted high
To the God who can make all things new.
Yet once more, I kneel just to fervently pray
For my prodigal, it is all I can do.

The trials that they face are too heavy to bear,
But they fight just to stay as they are.
It is us on our knees, petitioning God
To touch their heart once more with His care.

So, rest now, my friend, as the battle still rages,
For it is in rest you can quiet your heart.
A new day approaches with prayerful concerns.
You have fought your fight, let God do His part.

Heaven's Gain

Each day begins with my hope renewed
In my time to walk His path.
So much to do, but my strength is weak.
With His power, I'll do all He asks.

When did my eyes focus solely on You
And the home You've prepared for me?
The death and sin of our present world
Holds no longer since I've been set free.

This faith grows strong as You fill my life
With the truth of Your Word each day.
I fight the fight to show all the path
And proclaim what Your Word has to say.

Now keep me, Lord, at the point of Your sword
To give my all in this holy fight.
Set my eyes and heart on your pathway straight
While keeping heaven's beauty in sight.

When my life is spent and I'm home at last,
May those who have known me well
Say with assurance that I gave my all
In this life, just His story to tell.

Daily Challenge

Once more, the storm draws me in
As my day begins before dawn.
With pain so real, awakened now
What choices will rise like the sun.

It has been so long since we have been whole;
Our lives in sickness torn.
He keeps us moving toward His home,
And in peace, I meet this storm.

The world holds joy and pain each day
For all who walk on these paths.
Not knowing which will be given out,
We all hope for our strength to last.

But, friend, I know the pain that can be ours,
Yet true joy overwhelms in its gift.
Those days are turned by the lighter load;
To each, their spirit will lift.

So now as I walk, no matter what comes,
I rest in the God who gives grace.
One day I'll awake to a home without pain,
And I'll smile when I see His face.

His eyes will show love that encompasses all
With a love that is so pure to be seen.
Our hearts there will soar to heights unknown;
Through His work, our hope, now known!

Portrait Drawn

When you stand before a portrait here,
What is it that you see?
The artist did their best to show
In gentle strokes and colors sweet.

Yet the portrait framed is but a glimpse
Of a life lived through many days.
A perception held of one moment seen;
Knowing this in what you see, what can you say?

You see a canvas stands and walks through time,
For it is a portrait of your life.
It is God who plans and paints each stroke
On mountains tall or in the valley's strife.

I see my portrait changing in times like these;
He shows the lines that age has drawn.
With the world ablaze, how does it change?
His gentle strokes show our life's meetings at dawn.

Is your portrait showing the gift of joy
Or of peace that you walk in each day?
When you see it showing a love that is pure,
Stop to hear what others might say!

Memories Visions

Within the night when dreams awake,
These visions come softly in view.
Our lives' scenes played out so vividly
From the old times to the new.

A young girl so beautiful to behold
Still takes my breath away.
Her love for me and for her Lord
Has grown stronger throughout her days.

In my mind, I see her dressed in white
On her father's arm so strong.
To begin our walk down life's new path;
So in love like a beautiful song.

With years together, lives brought such joy,
And some pain has come our way.
Still living a life of her faith so strong;
Showing love throughout her day.

Our lives have been blessed these many years
As we grow closer to that time
When we will leave behind these memories dear
To begin a new life sublime.

Love's Legacy

Within my life, I have sought one thing;
Just to build a legacy for time.
It will not be with titles, wealth, or friends
But will be from my mountains climbed.

Each one finds a time for a search of their life
To show how they weathered life's storms.
In their victories here, they have memories stored
For who come after and follow the Lord.

My search now has slowed as life's time wanes
On its paths I have left for those I love.
Just a glimpse of my valleys to mountain peaks here
With a view brought from heaven above.

Our search for significance will not be fulfilled
In the riches we strive for in life.
The true legacy rests in the hearts that we touch
And in all that we help in their strife.

So, rest, my friend, then take up the quest;
You now have a job to complete.
Leave all those here who have been touched by you
With a picture of a life so sweet.

Nights Together

The day is done as shadows grow,
And the stars come once more into view.
I work my day, then rest awhile
Just to rise and meet with You.

Your words are strong and easily read
So they can live within my heart.
What a precious time when we can meet
In the morning for my day to start.

Our spirits join before Your throne
With my prayers for loved ones here;
To hold and guide them through the day
So they can walk with You so near.

My steps grow slower as days go by,
But my heart is strong in the fight.
We talk till dawn, then I grow still
As the light overtakes the night.

Soon loved ones will wake to start their day,
For each will have much to do.
The many tasks that I will complete
Stir a heart that is guided by You.

God Revealed

Today in the pace of your busy day,
What would you hope to see?
It is in that hope that all hearts beat,
And our spirit yearns to be free.

I often stop now just to look
At the wonders that my God shows.
With simple things that are rarely seen,
He unfolds that we all may know!

God can be seen in a crystal stream
As it winds its way to the sea.
His power is shown in flowers small
And in the storms that rage around me.

So often now, I spot His work
In the beauty of a child at play;
Or in a saint that has stood their test of time,
For His power can be shared in what they say.

Now pilgrim, rest, as I have done
To look for your God, who draws near.
He will reveal Himself if we stop to look,
And He will show us His love so clear.

Chosen Hearts

The call was soft to a listening heart
As each came to hear what He shared.
Some troubled or hurting, they each listened,
For it seemed the teacher really cared.

His choices were different as those chosen stood;
Most were just ordinary men of their day.
With fishermen, a carpenter, and others,
They saw the results of what He said.

A nation of God's people was suspicious
Since this teacher was not well-known.
Yet His words of love and compassion
Came to hearts where living seeds were sown.

The story of Jesus is still with us
As we live in today's restless world.
His calling of the disciples was so simple
Just so the story of Jesus would be told.

What part of His story pulls at your heart now
Where a decision to trust or walk away must be made?
He gave up His life, then conquered death.
Now choose Jesus; He arose for your sins to be paid.

Hilltop Renewal

Today from a hilltop, I saw Your work;
All the valleys and hills such a sight.
The trees were ablaze with such vibrant hues.
My heart renewed in the fall sunlight.

Oft times we look, but never find
A glimpse of Your face in our day.
We run so fast, never stopping to rest
Or listen for what You might say.

Our nation is torn amidst the sides so strong,
Never speaking in love of peace to find.
They shout from their perch for all to hear,
Yet it's clear what is on their mind.

With founders who fought for freedom's dream,
When will our leaders stop, then hear?
In the stars and stripes, there's a common thread
To live long in freedom and stop the tears.

On that hilltop today, Your face I saw
And heard in my heart that still small voice
That it's not in our leaders or laws to live free
But in Jesus and His work, our only choice.

Timeless Shield

With hurried steps, we entered in
To a room filled to the brim.
The only seats left to be filled
Were the two in back of him.

This aged saint had hair so white;
His brow, the signs of many years.
With face etched deep from life's long walk
Still in him, a glint of care.

Then asked to stand and sing a song,
I saw a sight so clear.
His Bible laid upon the pew;
Its pages worn and tore.

In him, I saw a sight so rare
Of a heart and life lived right.
With Jesus's Word, loved and learned,
This Bible was a wondrous sight.

Not for his gain did it lay there;
But his shield for warfare's fight.
The pages thin and worn over time;
Still, for me, a glorious sight.

I looked once more to this saintly man,
Then I bowed my head in shame.
His life was spent in serving Christ;
One desire was for Christ's gain.

His shield had held off many blows
From an enemy hot with rage.
But no blows were felt by this dear saint;
His safety in that well-worn page.

Heaven's Hope

I sat with You once more this morn,
As the light of dawn drew near,
It's in this time, my heart awakes,
And I am filled with visions clear.

This world erupts with passions hot
From the evil that fills our land.
There is no escape from senseless deeds
Done from sin's emboldened hands.

Yet now my heart is calm and sure,
For I know that my future is held
By the Maker and Giver of a wondrous plan,
Whose story must still be told.

For it's in this time when the sky burns bright
That I find in my heart such peace.
His Word and Spirit bring new each day
Those words that offer sweet relief.

If your days wax cold from futile fights
And you tire of doing things alone,
God's wonderful gift through Jesus His Son
Will turn your eyes to a heavenly home.

Morning Test

The world wakes up in its usual way
With beautiful colors to start the day.
It's a simple time where dreams awake
To begin our day, not knowing what's at stake.

In some, the time starts when trials come,
They never expect it, and their mind goes numb.
What happens now begins their test
And how they'll respond on their path for what's best.

I have been there before, and it's hard to hear
That still, small voice where God is near.
But rest will come as the trials wane;
Your heart and soul to never be the same.

For it's in the test that God begins to build
A strength and passion that will mold your will.
This world holds little, but here pain lives;
With all your struggles, look for what God gives.

As the Son shines bright and peace returns,
Look to your heart and what you've learned.
Our warfare here must be fought for a time
Till our walk here ends and to heaven we climb!

Love's Fight

I stood today amid my world
To take stock in the projects I have chosen.
Some seemed so important as they all began,
Yet now it's time to see some close.

The Spirit has worked in His way ever quiet
For me to put on His armor for the fray.
With time, now so short, I'm fixed only on Him,
Who will give me His grace for the day.

My family and friends, now drawn in close,
As our world spins faster toward death.
Not all here have chosen my Jesus as Lord;
I will fight for them till my final breath.

Yet some here have chosen and are there now with Him;
Their journey complete as they reached heaven's gate.
Still my heart is so heavy as I see battles toll;
My quest here is sure, and I pray I'm not too late.

Now soldier, arise, take your armor and sword
To battle with fights all around.
His Spirit will guide you for your family and friends;
In time, you can lead them to where Jesus is found.

Night Light

Once more, I awake to a morning bright
The light of the stars fills the sky.
Their beauty is seen in the place that You set;
So often I stop and ask why.

Why did You make such beauty to see
In this world where we get to live?
Your hands have created with power and love
From the mountains to the oceans, our gift.

For it is in nature, we see the finger of God
As You wove such a tapestry sweet.
In its beauty, we watch how all things entwine;
In life cycles, Your creation completes.

So why does man find it hard to accept
In this world that You spoke into place,
Where God is the giver and sustainer of all?
We need only to seek out Your face.

The face of our God is not readily seen,
But its glimpse is given in our world.
A love that is deep in its riches bestowed;
Just a hint of Your heaven we are shown.

First Day

The days have passed so slowly here
Since we stood and said goodbye.
To the man and son and brother dear,
Who was much too young to die.

Each day one thought comes into view,
And I stop and watch in awe
Of the place my heart so yearns to see
Just to walk the streets of God.

What did you do when you saw Him there
As He held you and welcomed you home?
How deep was your love for our Lord that day
When you bowed before God on His throne?

With family, there was your reunion sweet
To see our loved ones long gone;
Holding tightly to those who've walked our path
Now part of the heavenly throng.

We read so true that our vision here
Is like through a haze, not clear.
In wisdom, He chose to hide from our view
The beauty that would bring us to tears.

God's Freedom

Our world stands now at a crossroads
Where we look at directions unclear.
We have but one way open
To lead our families here.

Over time our country has chosen
In their own minds what is right.
But it is not how our country started,
For those leaders had a vision in sight.

A nation that stood for its freedom,
And that freedom came from the Lord.
They penned our framework in worship,
So how did we lose all that's good?

With hearts not seeking the true God,
The country has lost His embrace.
Those decisions will change our direction
When we follow leaders and not seek God's face.

So, stop now and look at your heart, friend,
Taking stock of what leads you today.
The choice is clear, for God stands alone;
He is waiting for us just to pray.

The prayer of repentance will bring God back
To a nation that is lost in its sin.
When we bow knees, and hearts submitting,
We'll find God, it's the only way to Him.

Homecoming Rest

I dream often of a time that will come
To each of us that walk this ground;
An appointment set from eternity past
For each to stand before the One.

His radiant beauty will surpass all hope
As we bow before the Son.
Our hearts will swell from the love He shows,
For our battles in life now are gone.

We will kneel before the King of kings;
With our tears and smiles He will know.
This thankful soul longs to see his home
Where God's Son has allowed us to go.

With a crystal river and tree of life,
No thoughts or dreams could hold.
Such beauty there on every side,
How could our story be told?

Yet now they gather to see us there;
Those at rest in the glory of the Lord.
In silence, they sit for a pilgrim has come
To share of their life in their words.

All valleys deep and mountains high
Have served to build that life.
So great was the test, yet now complete
To spend eternity at Jesus's side.

Choose Joy

Today a question brought a time to reflect
Amidst the trouble and joy in a life.
With all that's dark and pain ever near,
What joy can be found in this time?

I go to the Word and find my Lord there;
In His writings, it is easily found.
Our peace and our joy cannot be discovered here;
Only given by the Lord to those who were bound.

My life is in turmoil from earthly pains here,
But I walk every day in His care.
There is joy in my heart and a song once again
For each new day's pain the Lord helps me bear.

If you are held captive in a trial's icy grip,
Look to the One who gives peace.
When the Spirit draws near, and you open your heart,
Jesus enters and brings sweet relief.

We now can choose to walk on this path
Where His strength will surpass all we face.
Even now, I choose joy to walk through my day;
In His arms, I feel His powerful embrace!

Heaven's Home

Just as the morning light begins to shine
And as certain as the moon will rise,
One day we will all be taken there
To a place that transcends all time.

I know that when my heart beats its last
These eyes will behold all that's pure,
Where Jesus waits and His beauty shines
In heaven, where my place is sure.

When, in time, I gave my heart to Christ
And asked and received Jesus's gift.
My sins weren't erased but covered with His blood
That was shed so a new life can be lived.

In the book of life, there are names written down
That can never be erased or changed.
For the moment we chose the King and His way,
The ink on that page showed we are saved.

So, rest comes to me as I walk daily here
Just to see all the sights passing through.
A home waits for me, whose beauty I'll see;
Jesus and all there in my new home.

Morning Visit

I felt You here with me again
As the night saw the first ray of dawn.
Such a familiar time we often share
In the still and quiet morn.

Around the world, a rage runs wild;
It guides yet steals our hope.
Within the day, no joy is shared,
And it's hard for us all to cope.

Yet in this time of quiet peace,
We meet as You begin to speak.
That still, small voice gives hope again;
Your Word is the riches we seek.

I've run with the rest in times long past
To work just to hold the prize.
Still gaining those things, no joy was felt,
For things can't bring joy to a life.

Your words are the treasure that everyone seeks,
And they live now for just such a time.
Our quiet time here is a spring for my soul
To begin a new day sublime.

New Home

I walked today by a crystal-clear stream,
Just enjoying time in nature so wild.
These times are a part of my life and love
That my father helped build in his child.

Yet even now thinking of the beauty I see,
One thought seems to replay in my mind.
If the beauty of this world is easily seen,
What sights in heaven will I find?

That crystal river that runs from God's throne,
I am sure will cause us to think.
Heaven's purity shines from God and His Son;
Our mind cannot believe the beauty seen.

The twelve gates of pearls and streets of gold
Are a testament of God's love and plan.
So great a reward from the gift we were given,
Where our new home from God now stands.

But the beauty we will see will pale at the sight
Of our Savior as He welcomes us home.
His loving embrace and words just for us
Gives us comfort and peace from the love shown.

Finished Work

He rose before dawn, for the task awaits;
In the shop, it rests just for him.
His hands, so calloused, stroked the wood
With a vision of what soon would be seen.

This carpenter bent to work the wood,
For the project must soon be complete.
With chisels and saw, he finished the piece
Standing strong in the dust at his feet.

Do you think Jesus knew as He worked with wood
That one day He would be nailed to a cross?
In His mind, could He see a scene to be played,
Where His life would be given to pay sin's cost?

I see in my mind as He looked from that cross
A multitude that both feared and rejoiced.
Their hearts either burned that He soon would die,
Yet others would no more hear His voice.

That day on Golgotha, the carpenter died,
And a plan was started for all here.
His death and burial were the parts all saw;
An empty tomb gave all reason for tears.

Gifts Given

Within each life, a gift is placed;
It is given when they are born.
In time, they will look and find it there,
Wondering where it really came from.

Each will strive over time to hone their gift
To bring it to life in their time.
When work is complete, their gift will bloom,
Bringing each a new mountain to climb.

My friend, have you searched for your special gift,
Or having found it, you wonder what to do?
The Giver has blessed you but now just waits
For the fruits of your gift to come true.

It may be in the arts or in service today;
You can run or just love those close.
But once you unwrap the gift given you,
The choice rests in how it will be used.

When God gave my gift, I was blessed by Him;
And in its structure and power, I am free.
When I write for the Master to those so alone,
Praying they will find Him and their eyes will see!

Heart Unfolded

I went back again to that day with him;
We just sat and spoke of his life.
So many times, we had ventured there,
Yet this was a special time.

He spoke of things I had never heard;
Of his trials and triumphs then.
With wars he'd fought and his family dear,
In his life, so much had been done.

A love for country and deepened roots
For all nature and family here;
His softened heart was opened now,
And in whispers, he began to share.

In all my life, he had been so strong,
Yet this time he seemed so weak.
Those words he spoke brought hope again;
From his heart, he had chosen to speak.

You must live your life with one sacred thought
That controls all the things you will do.
If you take stock of the good in your life,
The Lord will lead you through.

For it is not in your power that you will succeed;
There is not enough strength to endure.
Look long at your life, then look to Him,
Where God's power and love will be sure.

Thanks, Dad.

Daily Fight

We rise each day to a world gone mad
From their never-ending fight.
A war within keeps most awake;
Little rest comes to them at night.

But pilgrim, we must raise our voice
To all who are trapped in this war.
Their hearts are ablaze from sin within;
What words will we speak with care?

If we magnify Him and rest in His love,
Our steps will be guided to the lost.
In the words we will share to a heart so in need
That Jesus came to pay our ransom's cost.

His blood spilled that day, set powers in place,
Where the stone could soon be removed.
Your freedom, as mine, was completed and sealed
When we asked Him to cleanse with His blood.

So, look out, dear pilgrim, and walk to the fight;
Our power will bring hope to those lost in sin.
The time you have spent preparing your heart
Can bring life when hearts are given to Him.

Houses of Light

When God looks down upon the earth,
What if He saw each person here?
As a house that is built on a hilltop;
Each, with one person living there.

The home some build are showy things
Of marble and oak and such.
They show the world their goals in life,
Yet their impact is not much.

Another home built on a hill;
So strong, cold, and dark.
No light shines out from in the home;
Fear stops light with its bars.

Still another home built high atop;
Its glow so easily seen.
The light flows out from every crack;
This life our Christ has known.

You see, my friend, you will build your house
That others can view each day.
The light you shine reflects our Christ
In what we do, act, and say.

My friend, the Lord has blessed each one
With the light of life in Him.
An eternity living with our Lord;
His light saved us from sin!

New Song

In times of trial, our songs raise high
To the God who has led us through time.
His love and mercy have brought us here
In our pursuit of a life sublime.

Yet now a fear and sickness come,
And our world slowly closes within.
Too hard to see that sun-drenched path
We had walked, never wanting to end.

But here we are in times so dark;
No good news from our leaders again.
What can we do to, once more, see the sun
And find our way in a light now dim?

It is not the times or events of the day
Where we will find those answers we seek.
The keys to the freedom and joy newly lost
Is a treasure not found by the meek.

Come boldly, dear friend, to the Father above;
At His altar, give praise to the King.
Your joy, once lost, will renew in His strength,
and you will have a new song to sing.

His refuge is pure and strong for all
As we come to a place so secure;
A love, unbounded, free, and strong,
To give us the heart to endure.

Heaven's Race

In each one's life, a race is run;
It began on the day we were born.
Our race is hard with danger near;
We run from the early morn.

The days all clash with others close;
Each striving to just get through.
Until one day I found the One
Who showed me what to do.

With Jesus, I've found the one clear path
That will lead to my heavenly home.
It's in His strength, I run my race
And not any strength of my own.

Now 'round about, the crowd grows deep
As I run for all to see;
A crowd so great and cheering loud
For me to be what He wants me to be.

So now my vision begins to clear
When I look at my future unfold
To a beauty so grand, it's hard to take in;
Heaven's grandeur, as the Bible foretold.

Choosing Thanks

The glow of the candles brought the room to life
As our family all gathered to pray
On this day set aside to reflect and give thanks;
I was excited for what I could say.

These days, now past, I have thought of the words
That would show how we all have been blessed.
In a world now gone crazy with violence and pain,
My prayer could bring hope and His rest.

Each day we strive to complete all the work,
But the goal seems to move further still.
Our homes are our respite for so short a time;
Within them, tired hearts can be filled.

So, what are the things that I bring here to share
In this moment so filled with His peace?
We all have within us every moment we live;
A choice to choose Jesus and be free.

With His life, He brought joy, healing, and love.
In His death, He brought payment for sin.
In His resurrection, He finished God's plan for all time.
Our choice gives us heaven with Him!

Grandpa's Treasure

The stairway was dark and narrow;
Each step leading up to a room.
Where all their life's treasures found shelter,
It seemed such a dark little tomb.

The boxes were stored there just resting
For the time they again could be used
By my father's dear parents and family;
These old things so much better than new!

It was here that I discovered that treasure,
An old trunk tucked away for a while.
Yet its contents, the jewels of a life's crowning;
The walk these two had o'er the miles.

A picture and letters of love's blooming;
The birth of a life through the years.
So young and strong in their commitment;
My eyes slowly filled up with tears.

The paper they signed when they married;
A testament of a life just begun.
Their yielding to each other all their talents;
Wasn't long till they had their first son.

Then my eye caught a glimpse of a treasure;
Way down deep on the bottom it laid.
Just a Bible, but yet something's different,
For I remembered the words Grandpa had said.

I have helped to bring you this far, boy,
And I will leave you my money and land.
But the best and dearest treasure given
Was watching you take Jesus's hand.

For you see, son, all the world searches
Just for peace and contentment within;
Only to find the same empty feelings,
The result of the lifetime in sin.

Yet this book gives the answers for problems
You will face as you walk through this life.
God's Word is the treasure to rest in;
His answers still fresh and alive!

Majestic Walk

Today the sun was shining bright
In the blue and cloudless sky.
In looking 'round, it was easily seen
All the evidence of why.

I often question, what is the cause
Of all these times in life?
Why is there so much sadness seen
And lives held down by strife?

It's then I sense what God has shown
When I see His wonders here.
From mountains tall to oceans wide,
With all the beauty and animals near.

So now I walk in God's wonders seen
Just to commune with God on high.
He gives me strength in time of need,
And in His strength, once more, I'll try.

I can't believe I've walked the miles
In strength only of my own.
But now I walk these paths with Him
Till I walk in my heavenly home.

Reality's Dream

Have you ever dreamed a silly dream
Just to wake and find it real.
Those sights and sounds so vivid there;
You felt you could reach right out and feel.

It happens now and then to me,
Never knowing when it comes.
Awaking to find those simple joys
Makes living life so much fun!

Yet lately the dreams I am waking from
Are not pretty or silly things
But cruelty and hatred running wild
From the bondage Satan brings.

We have it all around us now
In what we read and what we see.
No place to hide or wait it out,
And no refuge for us to flee.

It's hard sometimes to keep in place
Our values and priorities here.
For Christ to reign over all our life
Gives us reason to never fear.

Paused Power

What time of day do you take your pause
Just to think of what must be done?
It is in that moment that minds come clear
To see what battles can be won.

In all my life, I was raised for this.
For in taking stock, all things fall into place.
The clarity brought from resting and thought
Gives a clear course for what you will face.

My father was great at showing this gift,
And my life has been lived in its power.
For when we pause, the world just stops,
Giving guidance that is needed that hour.

So, friend, in your pursuits on your pathway in life,
Whose voice gives you direction and rest?
If the voice that you hear seems familiar and lost,
There is no hope you will conquer life's tests.

Rest now, then listen for the still, small voice
Come to a heart tuned to the Lord.
His direction and power let you see ever clear
That your path is much easier with His words!

Eternal Choice

Today the sun will rise on all,
For the Lord has set our days.
What happens today will be our choice
To go where we want and in His way.

Yet even now, some choose a path,
Taking them away from the God of love.
Their steps are made with a heart that is closed
To the God who made all from above.

Each choice we make comes deep from our heart,
Then we stare at the results that we face.
Over time we begin to move to those things
That our hearts have chosen to embrace.

My hope now, friend, is that you look within,
For each decision points to a place.
The life we live and our choices made
Give us eternal death or a look at His face.

When Jesus came, He opened the door
For each, in their time, to choose.
His blood paid the price, and His offer is sweet;
Turn to Jesus, change your heart, heaven chose.

Nature Walk

I stop often now to look for Him,
For He is so easily seen.
His Spirit rests in a meadow still
Or a river that runs to the sea.

My search has found Him on quiet paths
As I walked just to clear the noise.
It is in the stillness He often waits
Just for those who long to be close.

When was the last time God spoke to you,
Not in words like the thunder rolls,
But in nature's beauty or children's sweet laugh?
Not looking will never help your soul.

In the stillness now, He is always near;
Always waiting for me just to pause.
His Spirit clearly embraces in love
As I wait just to break down life's walls.

You see, He can be found in a heart that is still
And a mind that chooses to wait.
Our passioned pursuits keep us running all day.
So, stop now, breathe deep, He is never late!

Morning to Evening

In times like these, I look to You
For Your peace to fill my day.
For it is in the turmoil of my world
That I must stop to hear what You say.

Your Word is light to a darkened path.
In its light, I have no fear.
The time I spend in my study there
Helps my soul to keep You near.

My morning time is spent with You
With prayers and songs of faith.
Those quiet moments start me strong;
In their strength, I choose to stay.

Within my day, I walk this world
Like those from young to old.
Our trials and triumphs take their toll;
Still, Your Word must often be told.

At night, this heart and body ache
From the toil my day has brought.
With eyes that close to pray, then read
The living Word from the hand of God.

Wilderness Walked

The day begins like those before;
Never knowing what will come.
It is the simple and usual tasks
That we work to just get done.

And then a trial steps in with its test
To find if your spirit is strong.
You make your way on paths not known;
Many times, the road seems long.

What do you do when tests are hard
For you and all you hold dear?
Our life is anchored by choices made;
In your choice, the way is clear.

Within my life, many choices were made,
And the greatest, by far, was God's Son.
Choosing Jesus has brought such joy to my life;
Giving victories I could not have won.

So now in this test, I fight once again;
Yet in this fight, I know who will win.
The world is a wilderness just passing through
Till, in heaven, I will finally see Him.

Heaven's Gate

Each day brings news of events gone wrong;
Our lives are stilled through the hate.
Why do we stand and give much thought
When we could glimpse a vision of our gate?

Its strength and beauty are standing now
To welcome true pilgrims home.
They will look for those who have entered there
Where they will never again be alone.

I find my thoughts turn often to home
As I walk my way through this life.
One day I will find that beautiful gate;
Having left this world and its strife.

There are loved ones there who have passed before
To gain the home they were given;
In a place so pure and beautiful
And free from all forms of sin.

It is in that vision, I find my hope
Just to enter and fall at His feet.
Jesus will show family reunited at last;
In my home, in His heaven so sweet.

New Voice

How does your heart feel at His call;
With its stir, do you wonder or act?
Take time now to rest and listen close;
His presence draws you in; don't let this pass.

It is in those moments that few will hear,
For the pace of their day leaves little time.
Yet pausing now will give all the chance
To be in the presence of God on high.

When we take the time to watch and pray,
Our hearts can be tuned to His voice.
In the day's hurried pace, it still will work;
But each day, it must be your choice.

So, friend, tune in and join all there
Who, in study and prayer time and fast,
Have chosen to be ready to just stop, then wait,
For the sweetness and His power will last.

Your days can be full as your pace changes now;
Walking here but now listening there.
The choice gives you freedom to lighten your load
And listen as his still, small voice shares.

Published Works

I sat today just thinking
Of the year's last fleeting days
The time has flown so quickly by;
There seems so much to say.

A dream I had the other night
made our lives seem like a book.
Each day we live is a page written down
In what we say and act and look.

It seems to me a silly thing
Yet so vividly lived out there.
So many books lying all around;
Their pages written with care.

A common thread was woven through
Of their relationship with Christ;
The style of book pertaining to
His place within their life.

A mystery written hiding
The thoughts and acts of one;
We cannot be sure, but hope to find
Their acceptance of the Son.

The next all filled with tales so dark
Of horror, filth, and greed.
This life is seen so clearly now;
For Christ, they have no need.

Our final book, a lovely tale,
Of a true and lasting love;
With Christ, the center of their hearts,
A joy to read those words.

So now the year passes to the next;
I pray you will look within
To find the book you are publishing
And live your life for Him!

Heart Songs

The world around us burns with hate
While we walk throughout the days.
Our spirit tires of this daily fight
How can we surely do what is right?
Think on, **Softly and Tenderly.**

With hope held high, we join the fray;
Just being there causes us to pray.
In every trial, we see His hand
Gently guiding us to help us stand.
Think on, **Trust and Obey.**

What will you do to point those lost
To the Savior whose blood paid the cost?
Where the debt was paid, and each can claim
His salvation so they will never be the same!
Think on, **There Is a Fountain.**

So stand, dear saint, and look to those
Whose sin is gone, for Christ they chose.
It is with the choice you helped to guide
Their heart, now clean, rests at Jesus side.
Think on, **Amazing Grace.**

For each new day, our task is sure;
We will point those hurting to a peace that is pure.
They will see in Jesus's power and love
A way to the Savior, now above.
Think on, **My Jesus I Love Thee.**

Morning Peace

Awakened today to a morning bright
From the sun waking up my day.
With thoughts of things that must be done,
I stop, just wanting to stay.

It is in these moments I look for You,
Who gave me this night of rest.
This stillness lingers, drawing me near,
Bringing joy to this heart you have blessed.

Yet some will awaken to a morning cold;
Their sleep never brings such peace.
In hearts so hard, they search each day
For just a moment they can find relief.

The world walks past in anger hot;
Their fists all clenched with rage.
So many lives will waste away
From the angered wars they wage.

Within my life, I have felt that storm,
But a choice brought love and joy.
This battle strong is not mine to fight,
For in Jesus, there is peace in my day!

Heart Talks

I often go to a place where I stand
In all my imperfection just to meet.
The scene plays out in much the same way
As I bow low before my risen King.

His time is always open for this pilgrim.
For a time, we commune at His throne above.
Without exception, I come away changed
Because He fills me again with His love.

Have you gone to the Lord with a heart so broken
That it's all you have the strength to do?
It is in that act where God will draw near,
For His heart has a special place for you.

Why is it that we don't often go to Him
With the simple things on our mind?
He stands ready to meet us there
Where the Spirit and power we will find.

So now when life's storms begin to come,
I seek no shelter from their wrath.
You will find me secure, at the foot of the cross,
Where His love and the Spirit guide my path.

Waves of Grace

We met again on this ghostly morn
As the sound broke through the haze.
Their rhythm sure as they came ashore;
Such sweet music in those waves.

It's in those sounds that my heart was stirred
From the One who lives deep within.
His prompting soon gave way to joy
As I listened once more to Him.

Within this life, I have been blessed
From the grace the Lord has given.
Each day He gifts me with its power
To feel strength from the One in heaven.

As I stand and watch those powerful waves,
I am moved by the Spirit's love.
For the King I serve gives waves of grace;
Their power is from God above.

So, rest now, pilgrim, in your daily quest
To fulfill all the tasks that you face.
Your life can be a beautiful dance
If you walk in His waves of grace.

God's Gift

The young girl looked down
At her now sleeping son.
His breath soft and gentle;
In her heart, she had won.

Her husband came close;
They just looked at the boy.
Their gift sent from God
Swelled their hearts with such joy.

In time, they would teach him
All things he should know;
How to worship the true God
And a trade where he'd grow.

Then Mary looked once more
As Jesus stirred on her lap.
What could they teach God?
And she smiled then and laughed.

Their son was God's gift
For a world so in need.
She could not imagine
That, for man's sin, he'd bleed.

Mother's Love

The young girl looked down at her baby;
So quickly he won her heart.
His eyes so bright as he looked at her face;
It was love, she felt, from the start.

Her son was a gift from His Father
Who had never been seen here before.
Young Mary had never given her love to a man,
Yet God gave her this Son, she was sure.

In time, Jesus grew to be a carpenter's son,
And his hands worked with wood for all.
How could Mary know that the man she raised
Would soon answer His heavenly Father's call?

He left all to open the eyes of the blind;
And those infirmed, He was destined to save.
When Mary would look, she saw only her boy
Who had given such joy all His days.

Still Mary knew that Jesus now had a task
Where a mother's love would not be enough.
His Father's love gave this Son for a time,
Where a cross let Him return to God above.

Mary's Hope

The days had passed so quickly
As you made your journey there.
A census by Rome was in place for all;
To their homes, they would go with care.

With travel hard as you carried the child
Who would bring God into the world,
What thoughts of yours would you embrace
When, in time, your story was told?

Would it be the marriage feast,
When your Son began His work?
Or the times He had healed the multitude
From the pain that made them weak?

So many times, the lessons learned;
Then His trial and beatings shown.
He was lifted high to pay the price;
Your heart could not have known.

But now, the world knows what you thought
As they laid Him in the tomb.
Your belief was strong; He would not stay,
For your Son, Messiah, has come.

Heaven's Gift

In the homes around our world today,
We all celebrate Mary's babe.
From that moment then when she saw His face,
She wrapped Him in cloth and in a manger laid.

His words have rung through the ages past;
To today, where we can hear them still.
He lived His life as the sinless Lamb;
So in His death, God's plan was fulfilled.

Our hearts are light on this day of days,
For it's not of the cross in our thoughts.
Only the babe in young Mary's arms,
Whose lessons for life would be taught.

Still, on this day, rejoice, my friend,
Giving thanks for that beautiful Son.
The choice He made to give up His throne
So mankind, to the Father, could be won.

As your day goes on with family close,
I pray your hearts will embrace the child.
His birth, life, and death were given for us;
The precious gift that was offered by God.

Christmas Shadow

The tree's decorated
With tinsel and lights.
The scent sweetly drifts
Through our house every night.

With mistletoe hung
Overhead the front door.
A kiss for my wife;
I could ask nothing more.

The presents are placed
In rows 'neath the tree.
Each one wrapped in paper
So pretty to see.

The smells from the kitchen
Of turkey and dressing.
With all 'round the table,
Now time for the blessing.

I thank You, dear Lord,
For our blessings so great.
The love of our family
And friends are so sweet.

But most of all, Lord
I am thankful for You.
You left heaven's glory
For love of man too.

Your birth in a stable
Is told near and far;
The trip of the wise men
Who followed a star.

But Lord, there aren't many
Who knew of the cost.
Your birth on that Christmas
'Neath the shadow of the cross.

Heavenly Journey

The day started early
As they rose before dawn.
With food and belongings,
They traveled to town.

It was time for the census
As decreed now by Rome.
All the families in Israel
Must go to their homes.

So it was then that Joseph,
And Mary, his wife
Made the long hard trip homeward,
Hoping there for new life.

For the wife, called Mary,
Was now great with child.
She wondered what purpose
For traveling these miles.

But the Spirit bore witness,
Though the census is man's,
Their passage to Bethlehem
Was all in God's plan.

Emmanuel's Gift

Our home's decorated with treasured crafts
In the beautiful lights from the tree;
A picture of life lived out through the years
With a love that is easily seen.

We will all gather once more in this home
To thank God for His blessings from above.
Yet it is not in the presents that we find our joy
But in Emmanuel's unfailing love.

The name draws me in as I say it once more;
Emmanuel brings God to our world.
As heaven stood speechless, Jesus chose to come
For the message of God to be told.

His life was a vision of what God would do,
Allowing us to be given that choice.
In choosing Emmanuel, true life would begin;
If we listen, we can hear His voice.

"My choice was so easy when I thought of you;
I left heaven's glory and thrones."
"To live, love, then die, yet again come to life;
Through that life, I have built you a home."

Stable Rest

The lanterns and lamps made soft shadows dance
In the streets of Bethlehem that night.
Our trip had been long, and amid all the throng,
We sought food and a place out of sight.

"No rooms," they said, "it's the census—no beds!"
For all have returned to their home.
Joseph's wife felt the pain, and her face showed the strain
Of the child, who, that night, would be born.

"I know of a place, just a stable with space,
but it's shelter, and I will bring you some hay."
I thanked him and smiled, just to rest for awhile
In the back by the manger, she laid.

Many years have gone past, each one like the last
Since the night that Emmanuel came.
Still the story is true, and my question to you,
What will you do in His name?

That name paid the price, His one mission for life;
Make a way for those bound to be free.
In His tears and His pain, all His followers gained
From quiet manger to Calvary's tree.

Beautiful Choice

In each one's life, they make a choice
To walk on their path through time.
Some choices made enrich their life
And give them all they could hope to find.

The life that I've lived has given joy,
For the times from those choices are sweet.
Our day was celebrated with family and friends,
Not knowing what our future would bring.

For most of our life, we have been blessed
By the Maker and Giver to us here.
Yet some times were hard, and the hurt remains,
But we have never given into that fear.

Within our home, we have made a life
To welcome all who would enter and rest.
Their joy, as ours, would help us build
This home for our family that's blessed.

Many years have come and gone in our life;
Still, we have a sweet time to be shared.
If our Lord chooses now to give us more time,
Each new day will be lived out with care.

Mark Miles

So rest now, my love, for these years are a gift
As we celebrate fifty years on our path.
In you, I still see my most beautiful choice,
Knowing now it's the best gift that I have.
Mark

Seasons Together

The morning air is crisp and cold
On this bitter winter day.
Its view is one all painted white
With snow that wants to stay.
For me, I choose to wait <u>quietly</u>.

My life's been filled with mountaintops
And valleys dark and deep.
Trials and triumphs we have all gone through;
With the Lord, always there, us to keep.
For us, we choose to walk with Him, <u>always.</u>

The bride I wed was my perfect match;
A soul mate whose love has been pure.
She still is my love, my joy, my strength;
Her spirit and faith ever sure.
For her, she has chosen faith <u>fervently</u>.

Each season in life slips quietly in
As we age on this march through life.
The walk now seems labored yet faster in time;
Our prize for this race He will give.
For us, we choose to trust in Him <u>completely.</u>

So, rest now, my love, in the grace of our Lord
As more trials will soon come our way.
Yet know now, my love, that this path we are on
Is much sweeter with you day by day.
For me, I choose to love, honor, and cherish you!

Now and Forever
Mark

CPSIA information can be obtained
at www.ICGtesting.com
Printed in the USA
BVHW050007210323
660793BV00020B/127